Things that Sting

Brian Birchall

Contents

Do you know what it is like to feel a sting? When you fall off your bike and graze your elbow or knee, it stings! When you get soap in your eyes, it stings! When you get a bee sting it stings!

Other animals and plants can sting.
Here are some animals and plants that
can sting.

Scorpion

Bee

sting

sting

sting

sting

Nettle

Jellyfish

Stingray

5

Some plants and animals that can sting look harmless. In fact, they do not look dangerous at all. Their sting may be the only way they have of defending themselves. It is their way of surviving in a dangerous world.

A bee flying around a garden does not look very dangerous. But looks can be deceiving. A bee has a sting hidden in its body.

If a bee is attacked, it puts out its sting and jabs it into the attacker. The poison in the sting goes into the enemy's skin. It makes the skin hurt and swell up.

The bee dies after it stings.

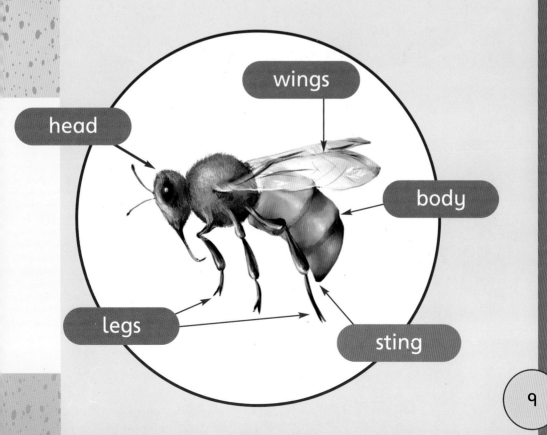

head

wings

body

legs

sting

Jellyfish

A jellyfish floating in the sea looks weak. It does not have claws or teeth or hard bones in its body to defend itself. But that soft, floating jellyfish has a secret weapon – it can sting!

A jellyfish has more than one sting. The stings are all around its body and under its mouth. The stings hang down like a curtain of fine threads.

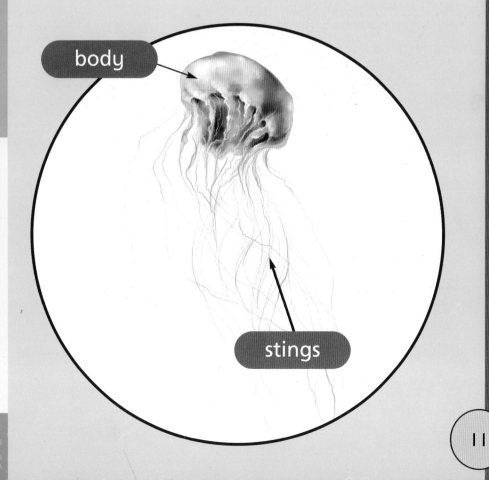

body

stings

WOMAN STUNG ON THE FACE BY LION MANE JELLYFISH

FISHERMAN STUNG IN THE EYE BY JELLYFISH

THOUSANDS OF STINGING JELLYFISH IN WATERS OF SOUTH WALES

GIANT STINGING JELLYFISH WASHED TO SHORE OFF COAST OF SCOTLAND

SWIMMERS STUNG BY JELLYFISH

JELLYFISH STING FELT LIKE BEE STING OR BEING THROWN INTO A BED OF NETTLES

If another creature swims close to a jellyfish, it touches the curtain of threads. Each thread lets out drops of stinging poison.

The poison is strong enough to kill a fish. It can make a person very ill.

stinging threads of a jellyfish

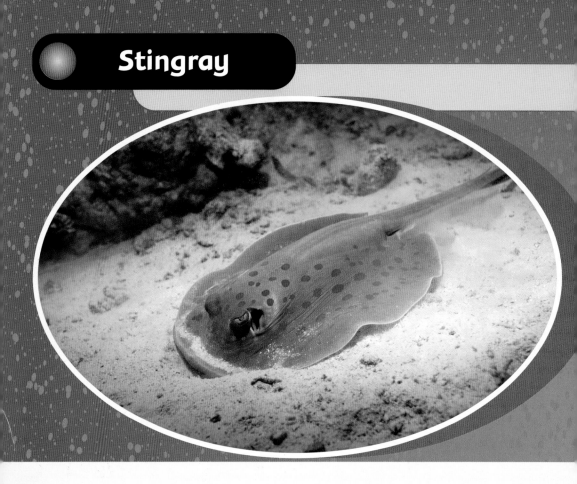

Another sea creature with a sting is a stingray. The sting on a stingray is a spike sticking out from its long tail.

The spike is called a spine. When a stingray is attacked, it flicks its tail and stabs with its spine. As soon as the sharp spine jabs the enemy under the skin, a painful poison flows in.

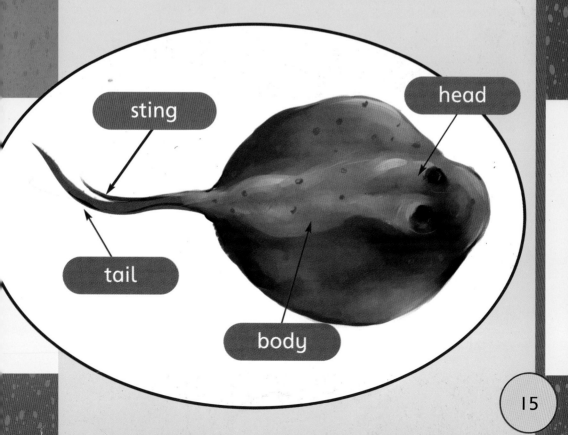

sting

head

tail

body

A nettle is a soft, leafy plant that springs up in gardens or in the wild. It looks like just the food for hungry animals to chew.

However, those soft green leaves do not taste as good as they look. Each leaf on a nettle plant is covered with fine little hairs. The hairs are as sharp as broken glass and give a painful sting.

Scorpion

People who live in warm, dry lands around the world should look out for scorpions. A scorpion has eight legs and two pincers like claws at the front, like a crab. It has a high tail that waves around and carries a very nasty sting!

A scorpion goes out at night. This is the time that it hunts for prey – usually spiders and insects.

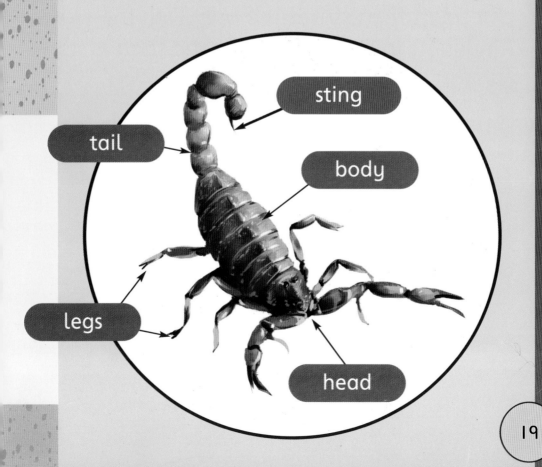

sting

tail

body

legs

head

When it finds prey, a scorpion grabs it with its pincers. It then strikes the prey with the vicious sting in its tail. The poison in the sting is strong enough to kill the prey.

This dune scorpion is eating a dune cricket.

A scorpion will sting a person if it feels threatened. A scorpion's sting is painful and can make a person very ill.

What to Do If You Get a Sting

Do you know what to do if you get a sting? This is what to do if you get stung by an animal or plant.

Some stings are worse than others. Some people have trouble breathing when they are stung. If this happens, go straight to the doctor.

Sting	Animal	Plant	What to Do
Bee	✓		Scrape sting out with fingernail. Put ice on the sting.
Jellyfish	✓		Put ice on the sting. Wrap with bandage.
Stingray	✓		Soak in hot water.
Nettle		✓	Do not rub. Run under water.
Scorpion	✓		Put ice on the sting.

Index